Oxford Read and Imagine

The Treehouse

By Paul Shipton

Illustrated by Fabiano Fiorin

Activities by Hannah Fish

Contents

OXFORD
UNIVERSITY PRESS

Ben
Rosie's brother

Rosie
Ben's sister

Clunk
Grandpa's robot

Max
Ben's friend

Alice
Rosie's friend

Bobby
Alice's cat

Now let's read this story,
The Treehouse!

'Hi, Ben. Hi, Rosie,' says Max. 'What are you doing?'

Ben and Rosie have planks of wood in their hands. Clunk is in the big tree with a hammer.

'We're making a treehouse!' says Ben.

'Do you want to make the treehouse with us?' asks Rosie.

'Yes, please!' says Max. 'I love treehouses!'

Clunk and the children make the treehouse floor. Then they make the walls and the roof.

→ Go to page 20 for activities.

Grandpa comes to the backyard.

'Do you like our treehouse, Grandpa?' asks Rosie.

'It's fantastic!' says Grandpa. 'Well done!'

'We can play games in it,' says Rosie.

'And we can sit in it and read books,' says Ben.

It's fantastic!

'You can sit in the treehouse and watch animals,' says Grandpa. 'Trees are good homes for animals.'

'Great!' say the children.

'Can I sit in the treehouse, too?' asks Clunk. 'I can find animals for you!'

Go to page 21 for activities.

Soon Ben, Rosie, and Max are in the treehouse with Clunk. Ben has his notebook and pencil.

'Look!' says Clunk.

There's a squirrel on the tree. It climbs down to the ground.

Look!

'What's it doing?' asks Rosie.

'It has a nut from the tree,' says Clunk.
'In the summer, squirrels put nuts in
the ground. Then they can find the
nuts in the winter and eat them.'

→ Go to page 22 for activities.

Ben points. 'Look! What's that behind the flowers?' he asks.

'It's a cat,' says Clunk.

'That's my sister's cat,' says Max.

'Oh yes,' says Rosie. 'That's Alice's cat, Bobby. He's watching the squirrel, too.'

'Oh no!' says Ben.

Bobby runs out from the flowers and jumps at the squirrel on the ground.

The cat is fast, but the squirrel is VERY fast. The squirrel sees Bobby and runs up the tree.

Go to page 23 for activities.

Alice comes to the backyard. She's looking for her cat.

'I'm sorry,' she says. 'Bobby likes to come here and look for animals. He wants to catch birds and squirrels.'

She takes the cat to her house.

Clunk points at a bird.

'Can you see that bird? It's getting food for the baby birds,' he says. 'Their nest is on one of the tree's branches.'

Rosie points at some flowers. 'Is that a tail?' she asks.

→ Go to page 24 for activities.

'Yes!' says Ben. 'That's Bobby's tail!
He's in our backyard again!'

The bird doesn't see the cat. The bird
doesn't hear the cat.

'What can we do, Clunk?' asks Rosie.

Clunk isn't listening. He's looking at a little beetle on his arm.

'A BEETLE!' he shouts. 'I don't like beetles!'

A BEETLE!

Clunk is scared. He jumps ... and falls from the treehouse!

→ Go to page 25 for activities.

Clunk doesn't hit the ground. He falls on the trampoline close to the tree.

Then he flies up, up, up ...

... and he flies down, down, down ... CRASH!

Clunk hits the trash cans next to the house.

The bird hears the noise of the trash cans.

It flies up to the tree. Bobby is angry.

Alice comes to the backyard again. 'I'm sorry about Bobby,' she says.

'That's OK,' says Rosie. 'But I have an idea ...'

→ Go to page 26 for activities.

In the house, Grandpa puts a little bell on Bobby's collar.

'What now?' asks Alice.

'Now Bobby can go in the backyard again,' says Rosie. 'Come on. Let's go to the treehouse!'

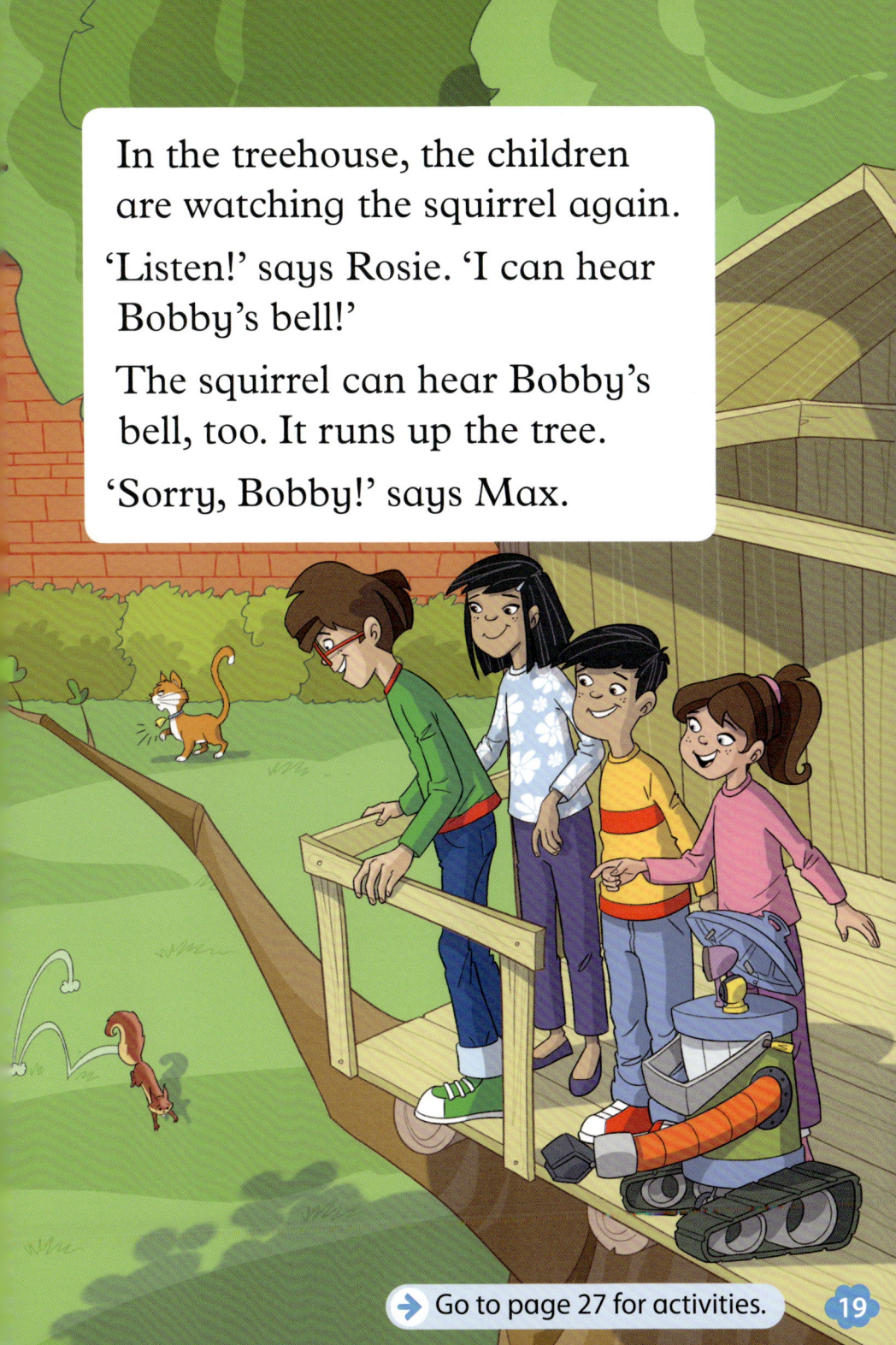

In the treehouse, the children are watching the squirrel again.

'Listen!' says Rosie. 'I can hear Bobby's bell!'

The squirrel can hear Bobby's bell, too. It runs up the tree.

'Sorry, Bobby!' says Max.

→ Go to page 27 for activities.

 **Activities** for pages 4–5

1 **Write the words.**

1 r a m e h m

hammer

2 n l a k p

_____

3 f r o o

_____

4 d o w o

_____

5 l o r f o

_____

6 l a w l

_____

2 **Order the words.**

1 and Rosie / a treehouse. / Ben / making / are

Ben and Rosie are making a treehouse.

2 in / the / Clunk / big tree. / is

_____

3 and the / make / They / the walls / roof.

_____

Activities for pages 6–7

1 Choose and write the correct words.

Grandpa comes to the ¹ <u>backyard</u>. He likes the ² _____. Ben and Rosie can sit in the treehouse and watch ³ _____. Trees are good homes for animals. ⁴ _____ wants to sit in the treehouse, too.

treehouse   Clunk   ~~backyard~~   home   animals

2 Look at the picture on page 6. Write *yes* or *no*.

1 Grandpa has some drinks.   <u>yes</u>
2 Clunk is next to Grandpa.   _____
3 Ben is in the treehouse.   _____
4 Clunk has a hammer.   _____
5 A bird is in the tree.   _____

Talk **Do you like the treehouse? Talk to a friend.**

1 Put a tick (✓) or a cross (✗) in the box.

1 This is summer.

2 This is a nut.

3 This is a notebook.

4 This is the ground.

5 This is a squirrel.

6 This is winter.

7 This is down.

8 This is climb.

Activities for pages 10–11

1 Circle the correct words.

1 A **cat** / **squirrel** is behind the flowers.

2 It is **Alice's** / **Rosie's** cat, Bobby.

3 Alice is **Ben's** / **Max's** sister.

4 Bobby is watching the **treehouse** / **squirrel**.

5 Bobby **climbs to** / **jumps at** the squirrel.

6 The **cat** / **squirrel** is VERY fast.

7 The squirrel runs up the **tree** / **wall**.

2 Look at the picture on page 11. Answer the questions.

1 How many squirrels are there? ____one____

2 What color is Ben's notebook? _____

3 Where are the children? in the _____

4 Is the squirrel up the tree? _____

5 What color is Bobby? _____ and _____

Talk **Do you like the squirrel? Do you like Bobby the cat? Talk to a friend.**

 **Activities** for pages 12–13

1 Match.

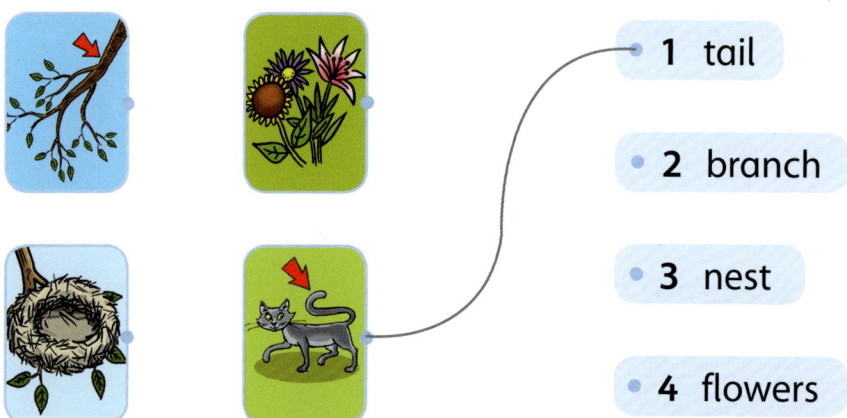

1 tail

2 branch

3 nest

4 flowers

2 Complete the sentences.

points getting ~~comes~~
looking takes

1 Alice ____comes____ to the backyard.

2 Alice is _____ for Bobby.

3 Alice _____ Bobby to her house.

4 Clunk _____ at a bird.

5 It is _____ food for the baby birds.

Talk What can Rosie see?
Tell a friend your ideas.

1 Choose and write the correct words.

Rosie can see Bobby's tail. He's in the
¹ _____ again! The bird doesn't see or
hear ² _____. What can they do? Clunk
is looking at a beetle on his ³ _____.
Clunk doesn't like beetles! He is ⁴ _____.
He jumps and ⁵ _____ from the
treehouse! Oh no!

beetle

backyard

falls

up

Bobby

scared

arm

behind

Talk **What happens to Clunk?**
Tell a friend your ideas.

Activities for pages 16–17

1 Write the words.

1 i o m p e l n t a r   2 s n e i o   3 r s a h t a n c

_____   _____   _____

_____

2 Circle the correct words.

1 Clunk falls on the **ground** / **trampoline**.

2 He hits the **flowers** / **trash cans** next to the house.

3 The **bird** / **cat** hears the trash cans.

4 The bird flies up to the **house** / **tree**.

3 Look at the picture at the bottom of page 17. Write *yes* or *no*.

1 The bird is in the tree.   _____

2 Alice has Bobby in her arms.   _____

3 Clunk is on the ground.   _____

4 Rosie is on the trampoline.   _____

1 Order the words.

1 puts / on / a bell / Grandpa / Bobby's collar.

_____

2 go to / again. / the treehouse / They

_____

3 can / the squirrel / Bobby's bell. / Now / hear

_____

4 runs / the / tree. / up / The squirrel

_____

2 Put a tick (✓) or a cross (✗) in the box.

1 This is a bell. ☐

2 This is a collar. ☐

Talk Do you like this story? Talk to a friend.

Project

Animal Research

1 Complete the chart.

~~beetle~~ branch flowers nest nut
squirrel wood tree bird cat

Animals	In the Backyard
beetle	

2 Do you know any more animals? Write them in the chart.

Talk What do you know about the animals in your chart? Talk to a friend.

3 **Find out about one animal from your chart. Draw a picture and answer the questions.**

> **My animal is a** _____.

Where does it live? _____

What does it eat? _____

What color is it? _____

How big is it? _____

Can it fly? _____

Can it climb? _____

Talk **Tell your friend about your animal. Now listen to your friend.**

Picture Dictionary

animals

backyard

beetle

behind

bell

branch

climb

collar

down

fall

fast

floor

ground

hammer

idea

nest

noise

notebook

nut

plank

roof

shout

squirrel

summer

tail

trampoline

trash can

treehouse

up

wall

winter

wood

Oxford Read and Imagine

Oxford Read and Imagine graded readers are at nine levels (Early Starter, Starter, Beginner, and Levels 1 to 6) for students from age 3 to 4 and older. They offer great stories to read and enjoy.

Activities provide Cambridge Young Learner Exams preparation. See Key below.

At Levels 1 to 6, every storybook reader links to an **Oxford Read and Discover** non-fiction reader, giving students a chance to find out more about the world around them, and an opportunity for Content and Language Integrated Learning (CLIL).

For more information about **Read and Imagine**, and for Teacher's Notes, go to
www.oup.com/elt/teacher/readandimagine

KEY Activity supports Cambridge Young Learner Starters Exam preparation

 Oxford Read and Discover

 Do you want to find out more about trees and the animals that live in trees? You can read this non-fiction book.

OXFORD
UNIVERSITY PRESS

Great Clarendon Street, Oxford, OX2 6DP, United Kingdom

Oxford University Press is a department of the University of Oxford. It furthers the University's objective of excellence in research, scholarship, and education by publishing worldwide. Oxford is a registered trade mark of Oxford University Press in the UK and in certain other countries

ISBN: 978 0 19 470932 3

Printed in China

This book is printed on paper from certified and well-managed sources

ACKNOWLEDGEMENTS

Main illustrations by: Fabiano Fiorin/Milan Illustrations Agency.

Additional illustrations by: Dusan Pavlic/Beehive illustration; Alan Rowe; Mark Ruffle.

The manufacturer's authorised representative in the EU for product safety is Oxford University Press España S.A. of El Parque Empresarial San Fernando de Henares, Avenida de Castilla, 2 – 28830 Madrid (www.oup.es/en or product.safety@oup.com). OUP España S.A. also acts as importer into Spain of products made by the manufacturer.